Flag of Baltimore
Adopted February 11, 1915

Let's All Go To
Baltimore!

Flag of the state of Maryland
Adopted 1904

*Written and
Illustrated by*

Kathryn Tanner George
"Caps"

Dedicated to my Baltimore family

Ellett, Pell, Taz
and Ace

BOOKSBYCAPS

Have you been to the Maryland Zoo?
If not, I have some suggestions for you.
Take a train ride.
Find a lion pride.
Watch the wood ducks swim.
See the lemur climb a limb.
Buy a souvenir and a snack,
Then tell the tiger, "Bye! We'll be back!"

HOTEL
BALTIMORE
BALTIMORE
This is For You
CAPS
WELCOME TO CAMDEN YARDS
HOME TEAM

Let's Go O's!

If our home team is here,
Grab your orange and black gear.
Then head straight to Camden Yards
Where Cal Ripken once starred.
Treat yourself to baseball snacks:
Popcorn, peanuts, and cracker jax.
See strikes, home runs, fair and foul balls.
Watch the umpires make the calls.
Join all the fans on their tiptoes
Clapping and shouting "Let's go O's!"

ALL ABOARD!

The B&O Museum is cool.
It's kind of like a railroad school.
Learn about passenger and freight transportation,
Diesel and steam engines and more information.
Climb all aboard and see what's inside.
Let the conductors give you a ride!

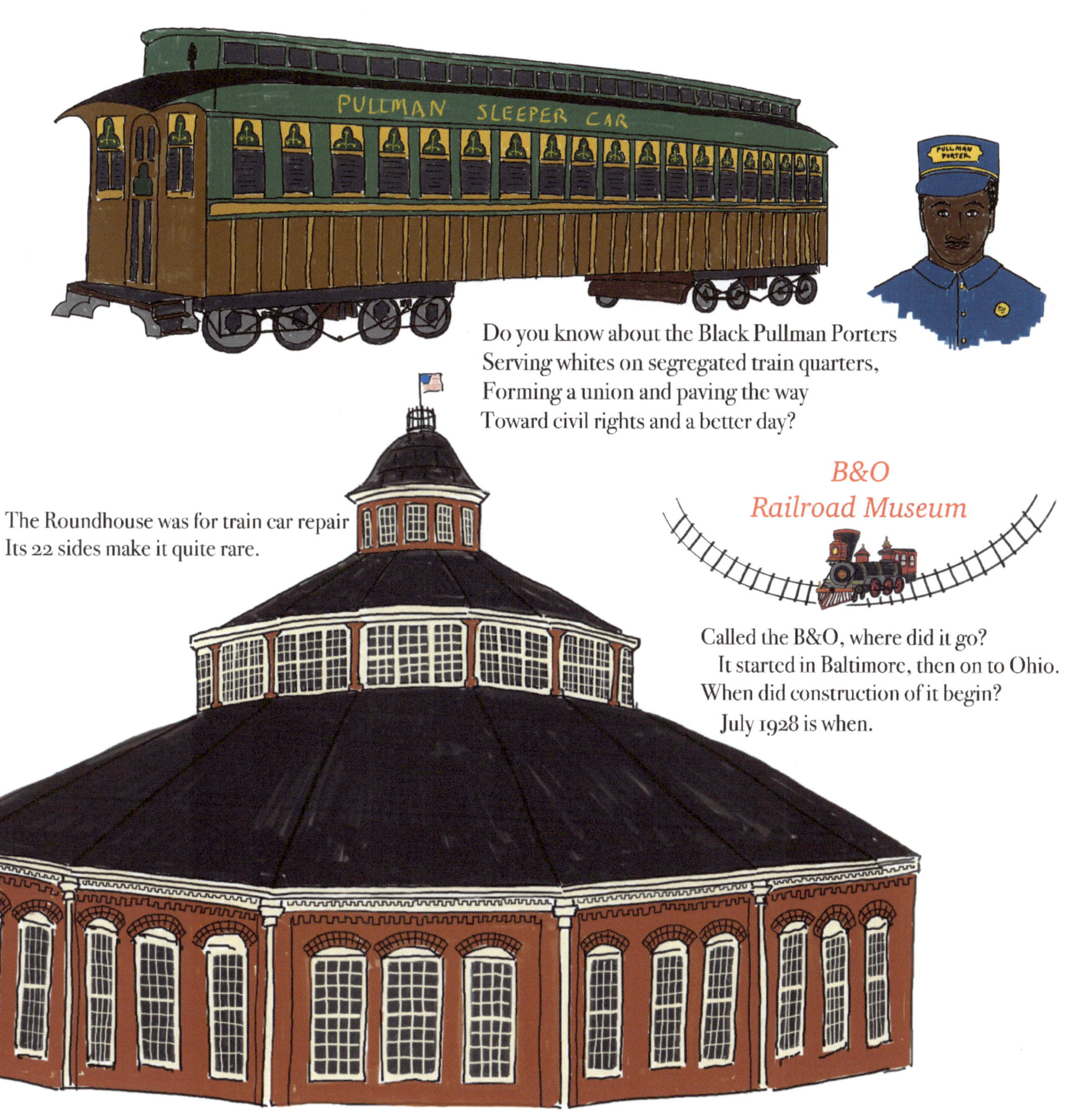

Do you know about the Black Pullman Porters
Serving whites on segregated train quarters,
Forming a union and paving the way
Toward civil rights and a better day?

The Roundhouse was for train car repair
Its 22 sides make it quite rare.

Called the B&O, where did it go?
   It started in Baltimore, then on to Ohio.
When did construction of it begin?
   July 1928 is when.

Who's Looking At Whom?

Baltimore's aquarium is quite exciting.
All the animals are so inviting.
Look each other in the eye.
Say hello. Don't be shy!
Fish, mammals, and reptiles too.
You might call it an aquatic zoo!

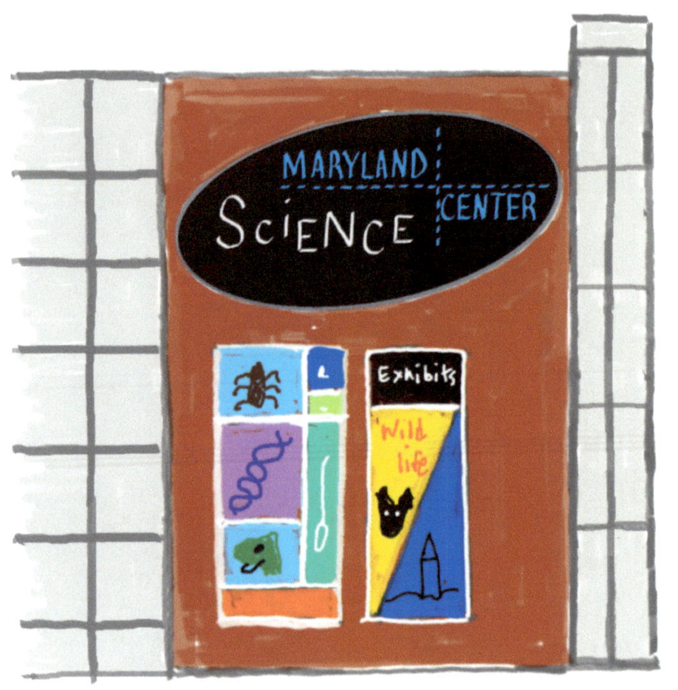

WHO LIKES SCIENCE?

After you visit the National Aquarium,
Head to the Science Center planetarium.
Learn about astronomy and outer space,
The difference between an acid and base.
See the displays of dinosaur remains.
Study the function of lungs and brains.
Everywhere you turn,
There's more science to learn.

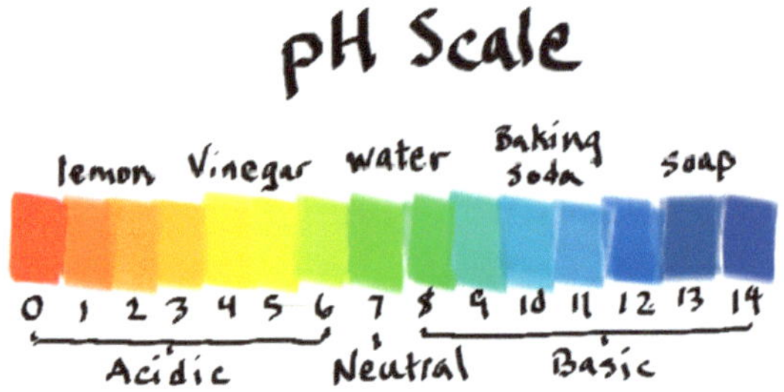

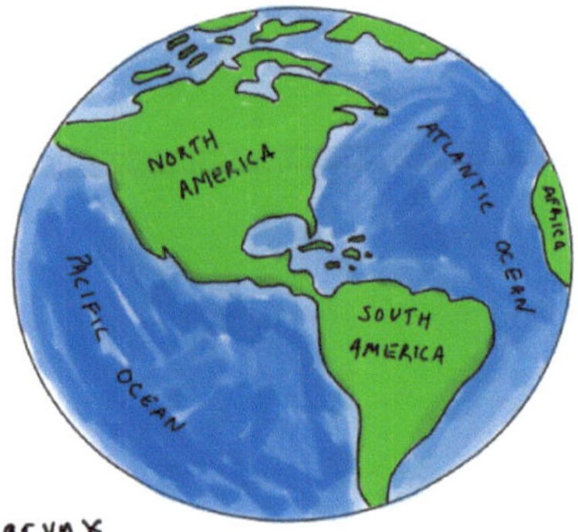

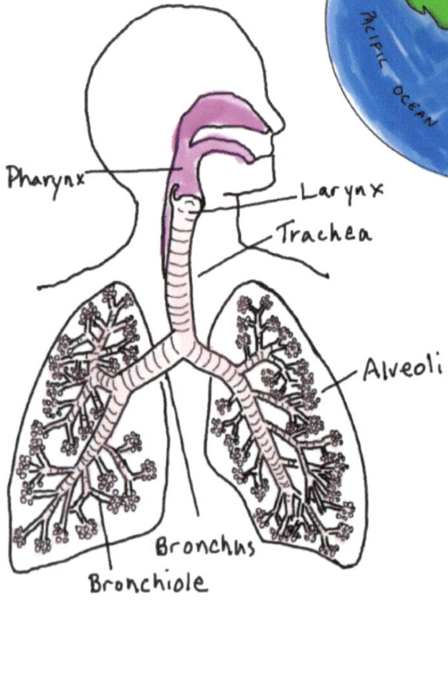

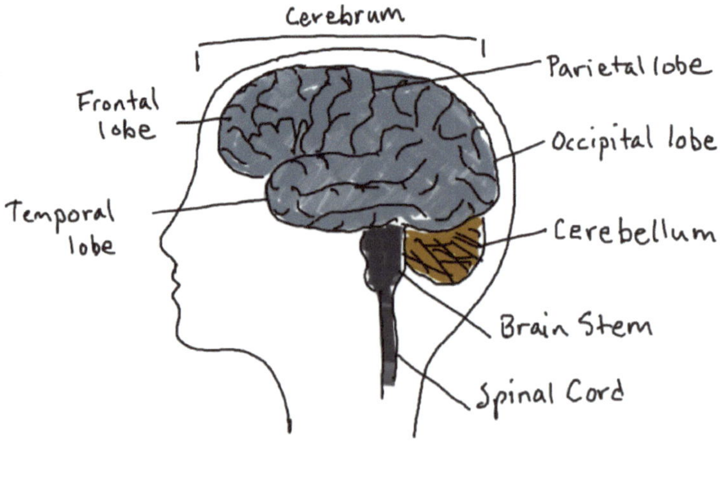

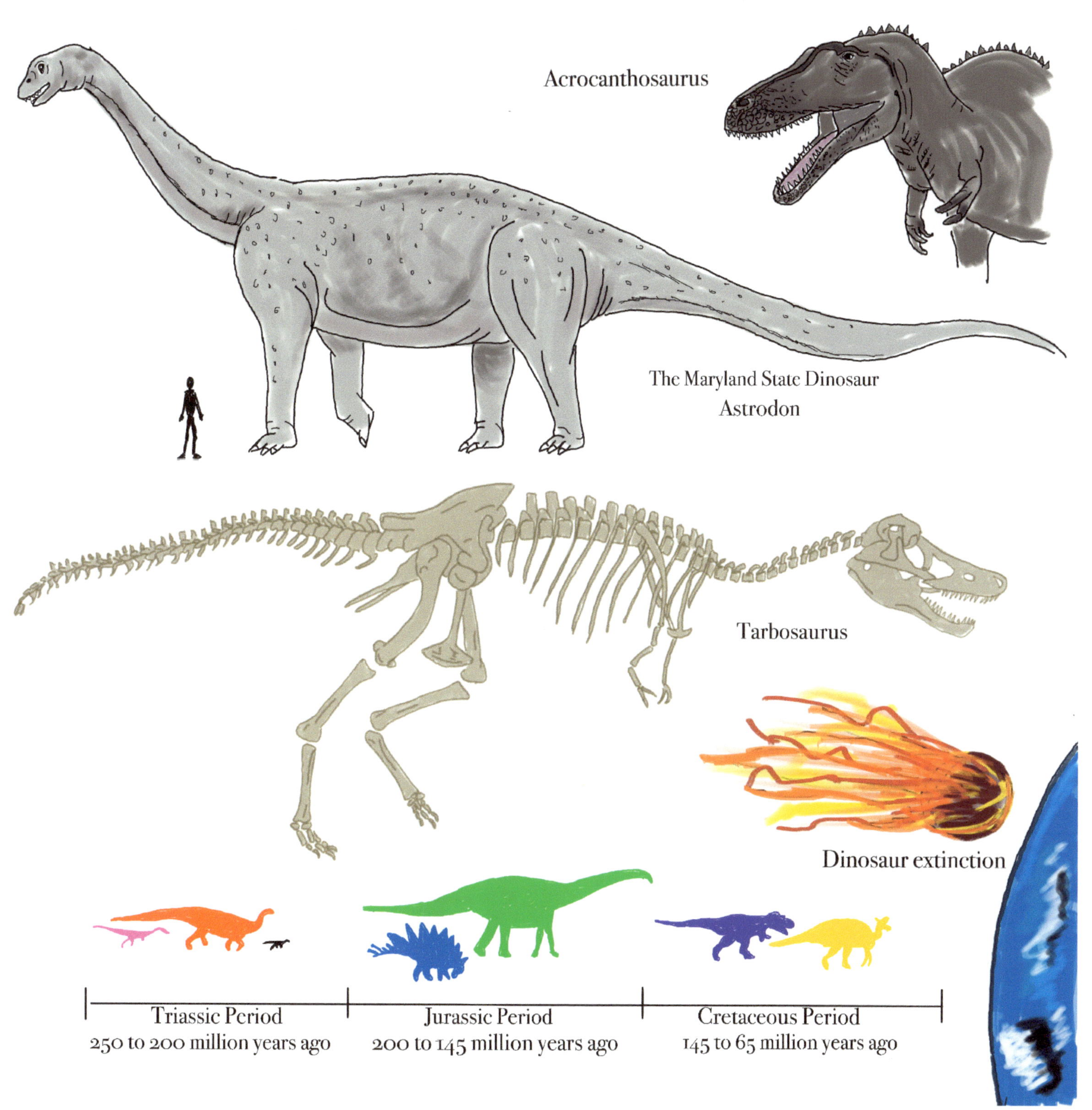

Acrocanthosaurus
The Maryland State Dinosaur
Astrodon
Tarbosaurus
Dinosaur extinction
Triassic Period
250 to 200 million years ago
Jurassic Period
200 to 145 million years ago
Cretaceous Period
145 to 65 million years ago

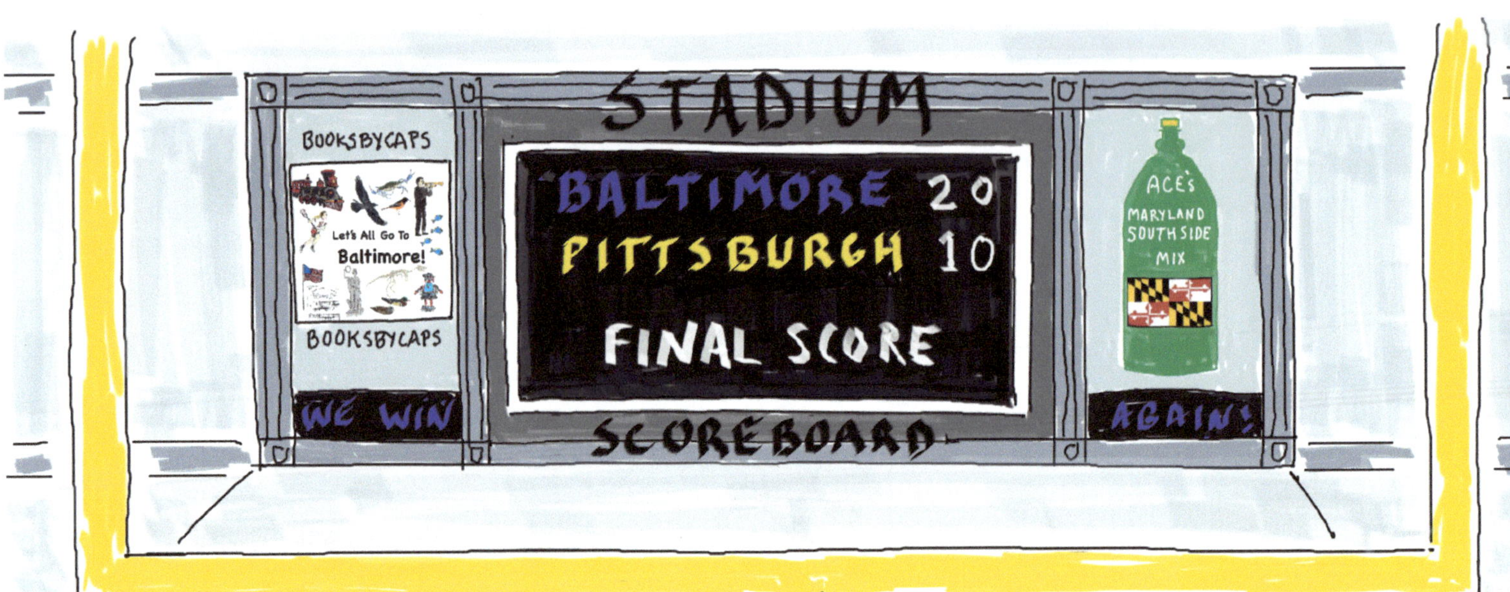

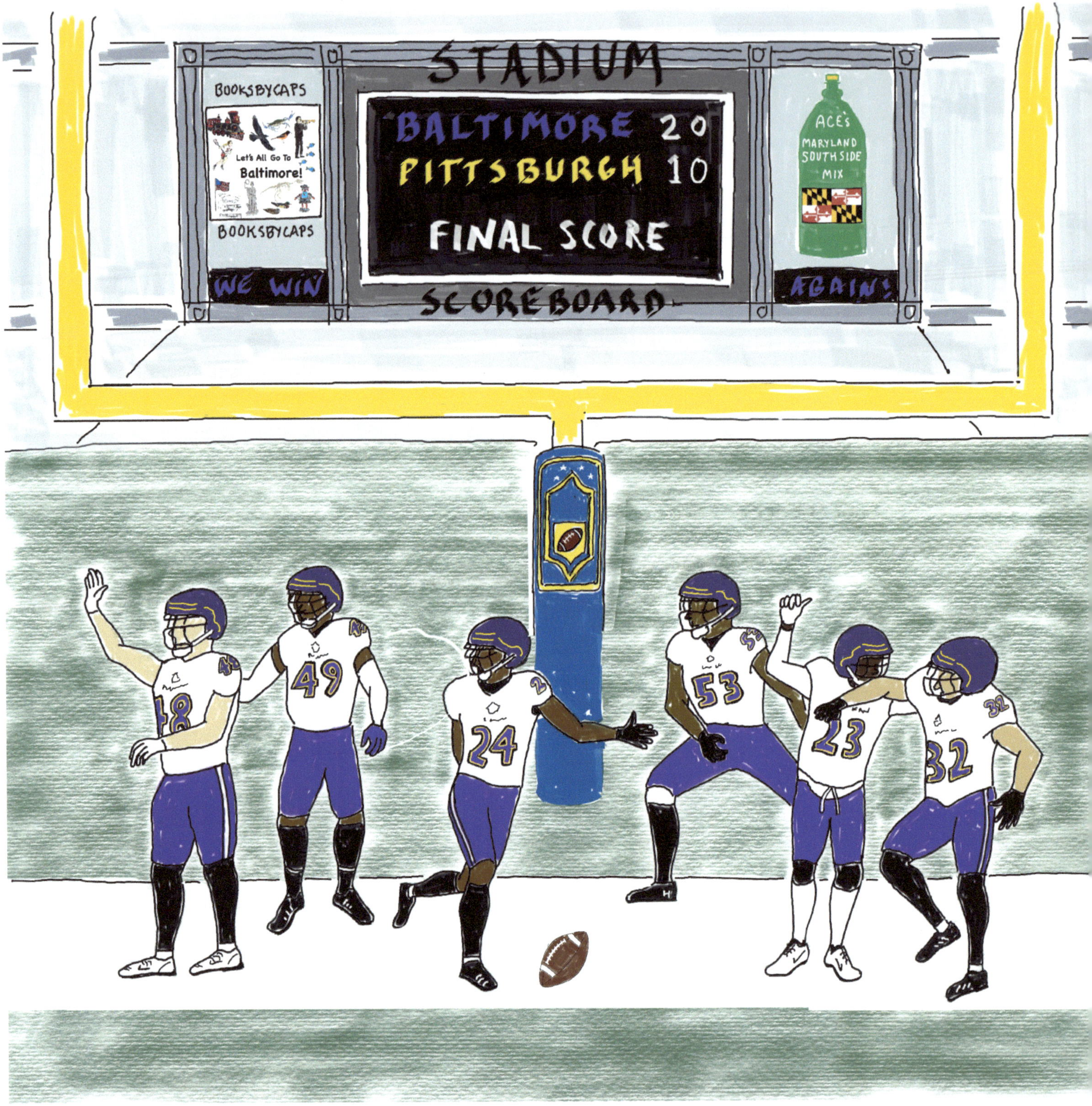
STADIUM
BOOKSBYCAPS
Let's All Go To
Baltimore!
BOOKSBYCAPS
WE WIN
BALTIMORE 20
PITTSBURGH 10
FINAL SCORE
ACE'S
MARYLAND
SOUTH SIDE
MIX
AGAIN!
SCOREBOARD
48
49
24
53
23
32

End Zone Celebration

Our team is home in Baltimore.
It's first and ten on the twenty four,
Looking like they're about to score.

Now see them dancing in the end zone
Where a very long pass was just thrown
To the receiver who was all alone.
And now their lead has just grown!

It's Baltimore twenty, Pittsburgh ten.
Looks like we're going to win again!

Matisse 1869-1954   Interior With Dog

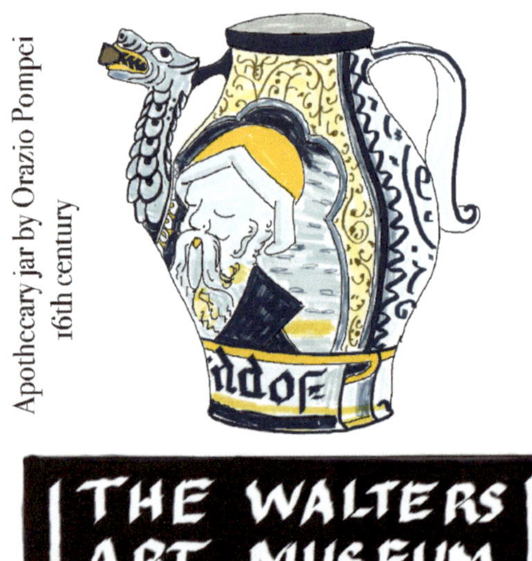

Apothecary jar by Orazio Pompei
16th century

THE WALTERS
ART MUSEUM

Piri Reis c 1465-1553   Map of the Black Sea

BMA

BALTIMORE
MUSEUM OF
ART

THE WORLD OF ART

Explore the world of Baltimore art.
Try The Walters for a start.
Glazed and painted earthenware,
Ancient books and maps so rare.
Impressionists at The BMA,
Matisse, Pissarro, and Monet.
The AVAM will blow your mind.
Every piece is a one-of-a-kind.

Devon Smith 1926-2003
Robot Family

The War of 1812
and
The Battle of Baltimore
Fort McHenry

The flag that flew at Ft McHenry
was huge - 30x42 ft!

O Say Can You See

During the War of 1812, Britain burned
Washington DC then attacked Baltimore.
In the Battle of Baltimore, Ft McHenry defended
the city and forced Britain to retreat.

Come visit Fort McHenry,
Filled with so much history,
Inspiring Francis Scott Key
To write "O say can you see."
Now read more about the war
And the Battle of Baltimore.

The flag was made by Mary Pickersgill,
her daughter, 2 nieces, and an African
American indentured servant, Grace Wisher.

After seeing the American flag still flying at the end of the battle,
FSKey wrote a poem called Defence of Fort McHenry.

Put to music, the poem was renamed
The Star Spangled Banner and became
our national anthem in 1931.

FSKey's original manuscript is at MCHC.

Baltimore's Washington Monument

Climb all the Washington Monument steps:
Two hundred twenty seven. Try three reps!
When you get to the top, I think you'll agree,
For a view of Baltimore, it's the best place to be!

Robert Mills was the architect for both Baltimore's
and DC's Washington Monument.
Begun in 1815, Baltimore's was completed in 1829,
and DC's 55 years later.

Cylburn Arboretum

Flowers, bushes and trees,
Butterflies, birds and bees,
Cylburn has all of these,
Plus trails and a mansion, sure to please!

And check out the new Nature Education Center!

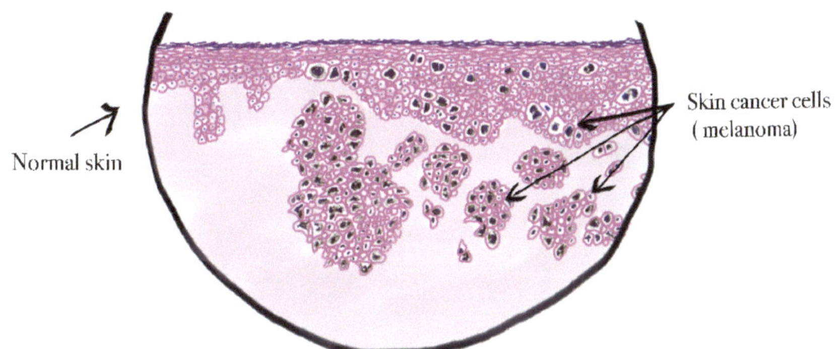

Microscopic view of
a skin biopsy

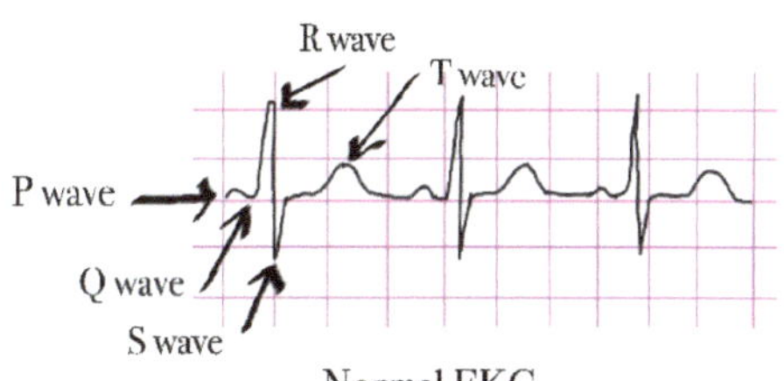

Normal EKG

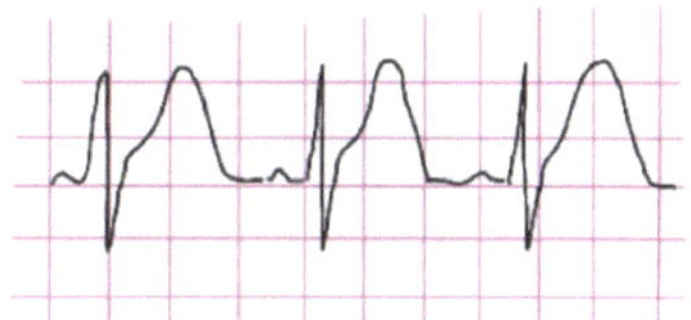

? Heart attack EKG

JOHNS HOPKINS

If you're really, really sick,
The best hospital to pick
You'll find on North Wolfe Street.
Heart attack, stroke, or cancer,
Trust me, they've got the answer.
Johns Hopkins just can't be beat!

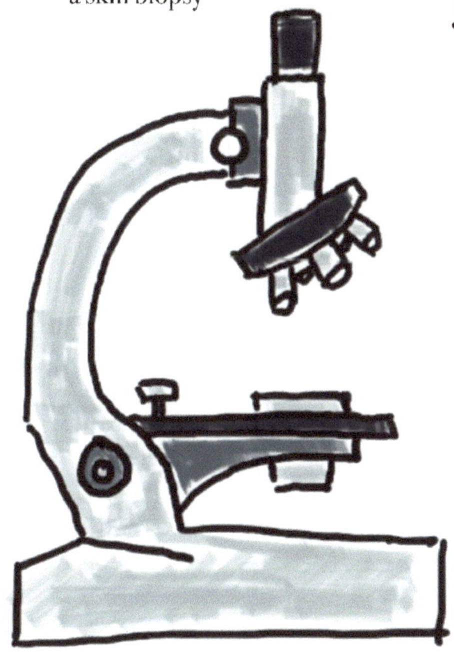

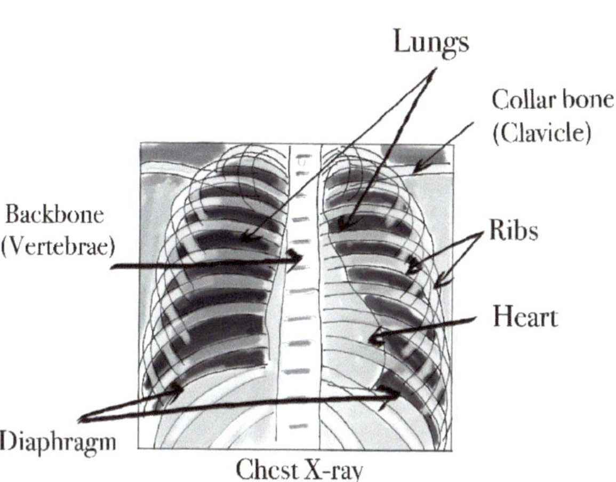

Chest X-ray

The Rod of Asclepius, the Greek god
of healing and medicine

16
Baltimore City Lacrosse League
Baltimore City Lacrosse League
Baltimore League
15

THE SPORT OF MARYLAND

What's the fastest sport on two feet
Where guys and gals with sticks compete?
With faceoffs, clears, pushes, goals,
Cross-checks, middies, and long poles,
First played by Native Americans,
Now it's the sport of Maryland. *
LACROSSE!

*Actually, the official sport of Maryland is
jousting, but in 2004, lacrosse was made the
official TEAM sport of Maryland

Portrait of First Lady Michelle Obama
National Portrait Gallery 2018
By
Amy Sherald
1973 -
Artist

Reginald F Lewis Museum Of Maryland African American History & Culture

Artists, musicians, scientists and writers
Statesmen, leaders and civil rights fighters.
All African Americans from our great state,
Whom we can honor and celebrate.

Dr. Nathan Carter 1936 - 2004
Director of the Morgan State University Choir

Harriet Tubman
~ 1822 - 1913
Abolitionist, activist

Frederick Douglass
1817(18) - 1895
Abolitionist, author, statesman

D. Watkins
1980 -
New York Times bestselling author,
activist, educator

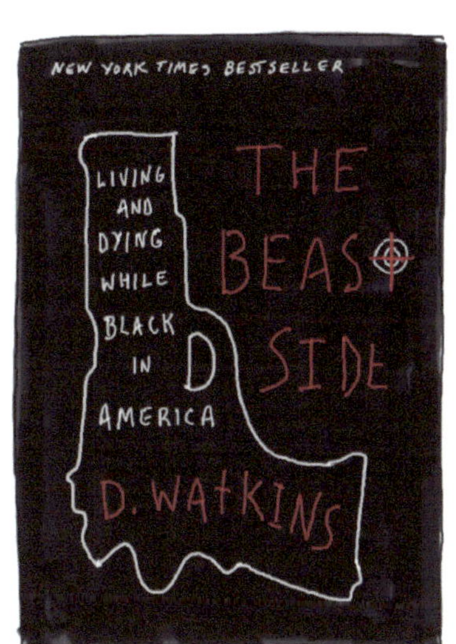

Benjamin Banneker
1731 - 1806
Scientist, astronomer,
surveyor, almanac author

Thurgood Marshall
1908 - 1993
First African American Supreme Court Justice

Baltimore Album Quilt
1850
By Mrs Josiah Goodman

WE LOVE HISTORY!

Bring your family to MCHC.
For history and culture, it's the place to be.
So many collections,
You'll love the selections.
Quilts, fashion, and Lady Baltimore displayed.
Silver and furniture, Maryland made.
Exhibits of African American life,
Both the progress and continuing strife.

Jim Henson and the muppets

Benjamin Latrobe designed
chair 1809

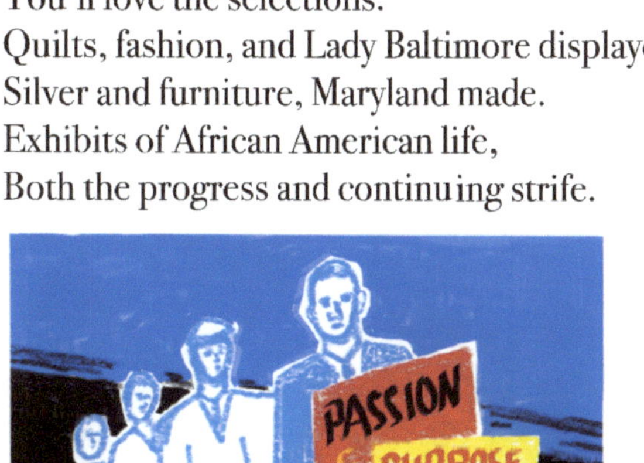

Margaretta Howard Ridgely's
Dress 1868

Claire McCardell
Designed
Dress 1955

Lady Baltimore

Race Day

We're off to see a steeplechase race,
Where horses jump fences at a very fast pace.
All of the jockeys will try to keep up,
As fans cheer them on at the Maryland Hunt Cup!
My Lady's Manor, Legacy Chase, Grand National too -
Such beautiful landscapes, what a view!

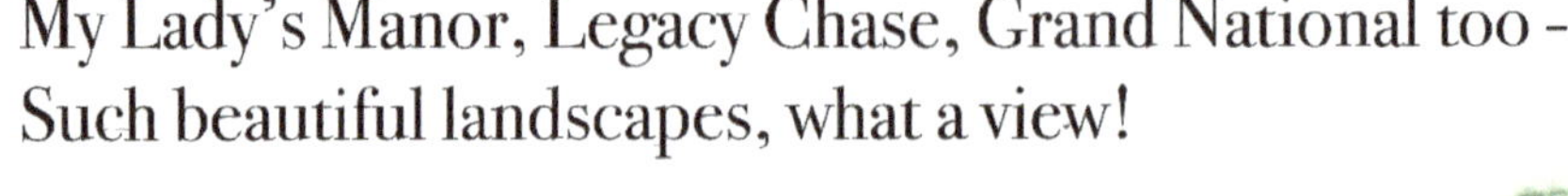

PLACE YOUR BETS!

Next, the best thoroughbreds come to town
For the second race of the Triple Crown.
It's the Preakness Stakes at Pimlico Track.
Let's see which horse breaks from the pack!

PIMLICO
Home of the Preakness

LISTEN UP!

You should buy tickets to the BSO
And Shriver Hall Concert Series also.
Hear the violin, trumpet, and cello,
The saxophone, clarinet, and oboe,
Along with the flute, harp, and piano.
And if you really want to become a pro,
Peabody Institute is the place to go.

OLD BAY
SEASONING
For Seafood
Poultry, Salads,
Meats
NET WT 6 OZ
Faidley
Lexington Market
Jimmy's
FAMOUS
SEAFOOD
CROSS
STREET
MARKET
Federal Hill

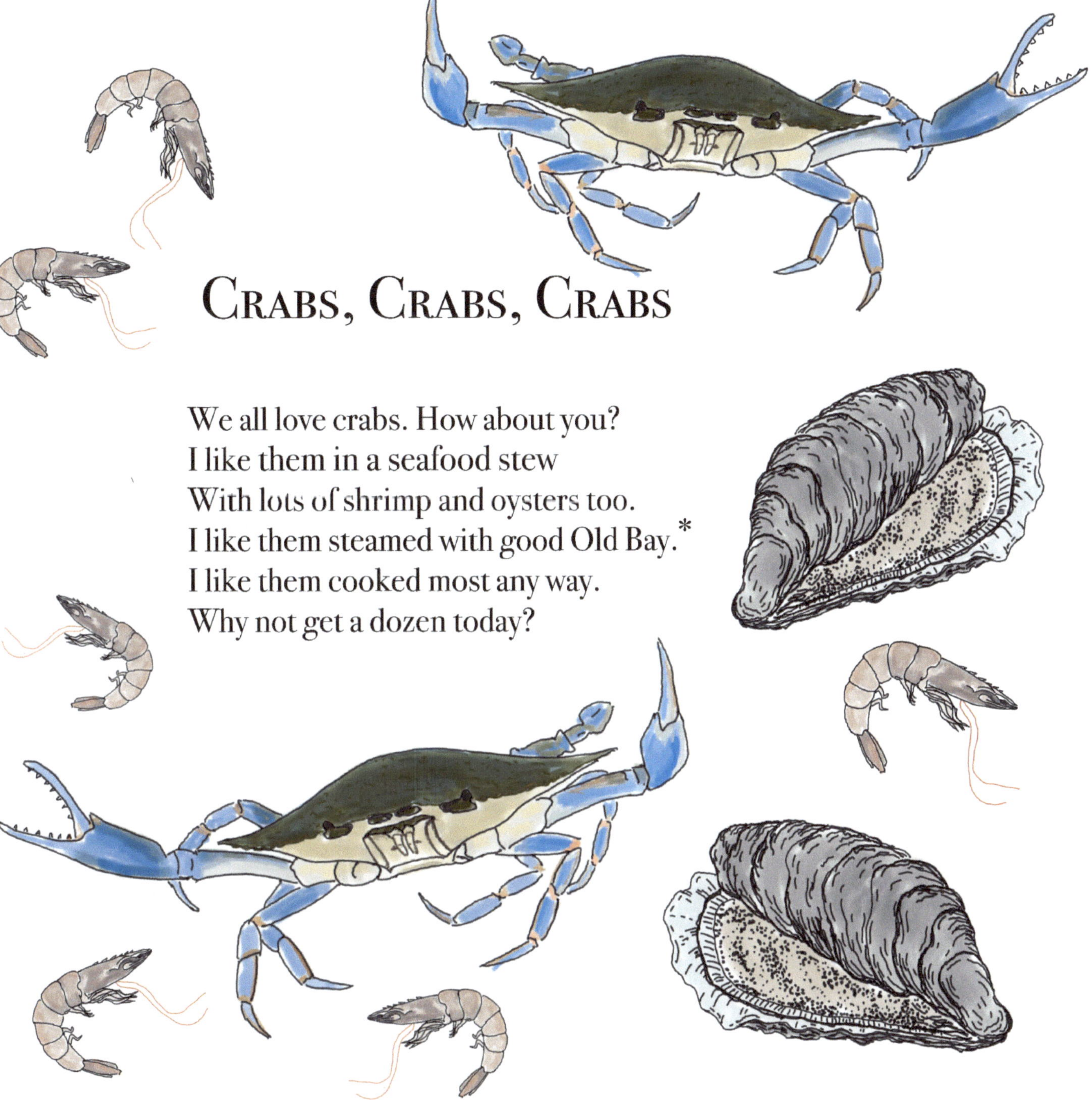

CRABS, CRABS, CRABS

We all love crabs. How about you?
I like them in a seafood stew
With lots of shrimp and oysters too.
I like them steamed with good Old Bay.*
I like them cooked most any way.
Why not get a dozen today?

Lightship Chesapeake

USS Constellation

Historic Ships at the Inner Harbor

The Lighthouse's job was guiding.
The Submarine was always hiding.
The Constellation was good at gliding.
The Lightening kept ships from colliding.
The Cutter kept people law abiding.

Knoll Lighthouse

USCG Cutter 37

USS Torsk Submarine

THE BALTIMORE FARMERS' MARKET

Every Sunday morning come downtown
To the best farmers' market around,
Where baked goods, crafts, and flowers abound.
Buy fruit and vegetables by the pound,
And a juice or coffee. How's that sound?

The Babe Ruth Museum

Port Discovery Children's Museum

The Hippodrome Theatre

Edgar Allan Poe
House
and Graves

More To See and Do

What else can you see? Where else can you go?
Why not the Hippodrome and Center Stage for a show?
Or the house and graves of Edgar Allan Poe?

And visit Port Discovery also.
Then see which Blacks in wax you know.
Go learn about Babe Ruth as a pro.
You can do it all. Just take it slow!

Center Stage

The National Great Blacks In Wax Museum

THE END

That's the end of these pictures and rhymes
Highlighting the best of Baltimore's times.
So many places, where do you start?
Museums of history, science and art,
An aquarium, sports, music and zoo,
The harbor and gardens, plus seafood too.
Make it a start, not the end.
Come to Baltimore, and bring a friend!

Acknowledgements

Thanks to all of the following for varying degrees of encouragement, advice, suggestions, and criticism:

Betsy B. the t-shirt lady and role model in every way; Hannah B. my connector; Pell and Nancy T. unconditional fans and cheerleaders; Clinton D. fellow retiree devoted to Baltimore; McCord R. practical consultant with an eagle eye and family discount; Diana D. nothing but positive; Mike R. best paying customer; Suzanne T.C. children's book colleague and cuz; and Wynn T. a combination of everything.

To Wynn Tanner, the real artist in the family, for permission to copy her 6x12 ft aquarium mosaic, Who's Looking at Who?, on display at Arbor Acres in Winston Salem, NC.

And to my Baltimore family, Ellett, Pell, Taz, and Ace, for supporting me 100% in my first career, and (with a touch of bemusement) in this second pseudo career, which has been nothing but fun! I love you.

In the spirit of this book and its support of Baltimore, the net proceeds of Let's All Go To Baltimore! will be contributed to the Baltimore Community Foundation.

About the Author

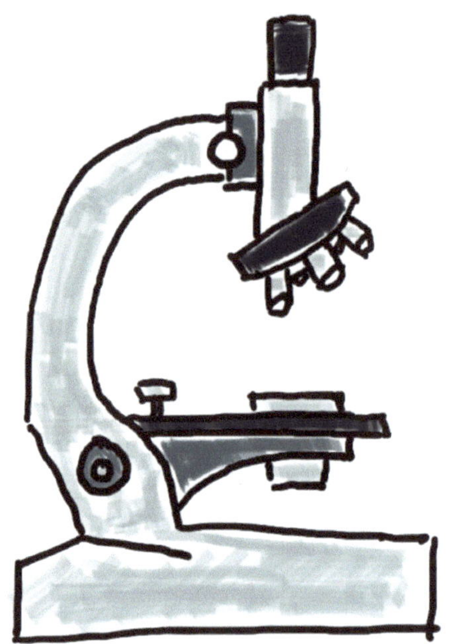

Kathryn Tanner George (known as "Caps" by her grandchildren) lives in Baltimore with her husband "Ace", where she practiced pathology for 35 years and helped raise their three children.

After retiring as a pathologist, she traded her microscope for an iPad and Apple pen, and started writing books for her three grandchildren.

She grew up in Rutherfordton, North Carolina. This book reflects her love and hope for Baltimore, which she calls home.

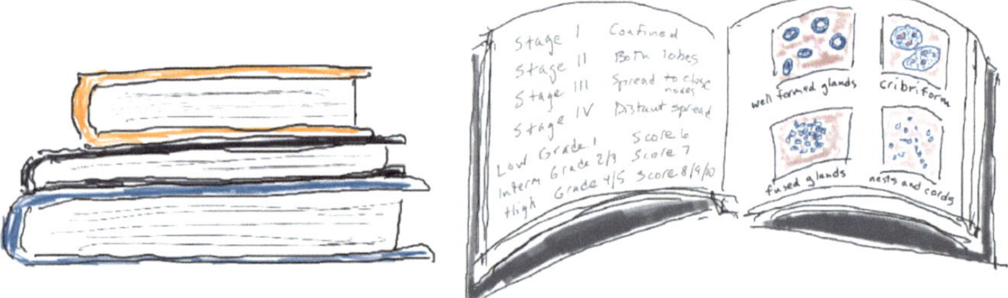

Tools as a pathologist

Tools as a writer/artist

www.ingramcontent.com/pod-product-compliance
Lightning Source LLC
Chambersburg PA
CBHW042054110726
48006CB00002B/395